*Good Morning—Midnight—*

Good Morning—Midnight—
I'm coming Home—
Day—got tired of Me—
How could I—of Him?

Sunshine was a sweet place—
I liked to stay—
But Morn—didn't want me—now—
So—Goodnight—Day!

I can look—can't I—
When the East is Red?
The Hills—have a way—then—
That puts the Heart—abroad—

You—are not so fair—Midnight—
I chose—Day—
But—please take a little Girl—
He turned away!

*Emily Dickinson c. 1862*

# *Good Morning—Midnight—*

## Kim Rosenfield

ROOF BOOKS
NEW YORK

ISBN: 1-931824-01-0
Library of Congress Catalog Card No.: 2001095407

Cover design by Jean Foos.
Cover drawing: Christopher Hocking,
"The Black Veil," gum transfer lithograph, gouache.
Author photo by Tim Davis.

Thank you to the following editors and publishers where parts of *Good Morning—Midnight—* first appeared: *Torque, Object, I Am A Child (Anthology), Mirage*. Also thanks to the editors of *Leave Books* for publishing *Rx* and *cool clean chemistry* and to *Object Editions/p o e t s c o o p* for publishing *A Self-Guided Walk* as chapbooks. Gratitude to Brian Kim Stefans for master-minding parts of *Verbali* as a virtual chapbook for *www.Arras.net* and for poetic tech support.

Morning and Midnight thanks to: Jean Foos, Tim Davis, Dirk Rowntree, Sally Silvers, Bruce Andrews, Judith Goldman.

*For Rob & Coco Always*
*All of My Love— To You.*

 This book was made possible, in part, by a grant from the New York State Council on the Arts.

NYSCA

ROOF BOOKS
are published by
Segue Foundation
303 East 8th Street
New York, NY 10009
www.segue.org

# CONTENTS

# MAXIMUM SAPIENS

# COOL CLEAN CHEMISTRY

## *CEPHALIC INDEX*

Sanskrit, Zend, and Greek
Goth, Saxon, Alemanni, and Frank
broad-heads make their appearance among the long-heads.

Turkestan, Afghanistan, and Kafiristan
The Hindoo-Koosh-Pamir theory
"somewhere in Asia."

(These broad-skulled immigrants have been absorbed by a long-skulled
population, just as the long-headed Alemanni have been absorbed by the
older broad-heads.)

Evidence of the Existence of 4 Races of Man:

1) blond long-heads of tall stature
2) brunet broad-heads of short stature
3) mongoloid brunet broad-heads of short stature
4) brunet long-heads of tall stature

And the inhabitants of the localities which lies between these foci, such
as short blond long-heads and tall brunet short-heads, and long-heads.
The blond long-heads, the brunet broad-heads, and the brunet long-
heads have existed in Europe throughout historic times.

The blond long-heads of Europe speak, or have spoken Lithuanian, Teutonic, or Celtic dialects, the brunet broad-heads once spoke the Ligurian and Rhaetic dialects. The brunet long-heads of Spain and France appear to have used Euskarian, what they spoke in the Mediterranean islands and Southern Italy does not appear.

Their country lies between that of the tall, blond long-heads on the north, that of the short, brunet broad-heads on the west, and that of the tall, brunet long-heads of the east.

# THE SAND-RECKONER

*throw out nature with a pitchfork and back she comes*


The heart is the special seat of life
a globe which whirls by force of steam,
lemon, and syrup.

Lapidaries and herbals
Wandering scholars
Alizarin, borax, elixir, natron, talc, and tartar.

The New Moon in the arms of the Old
Earthshine
Calculus, the glory of Leibnitz.

Fessonia
Uterina (guard of the womb)
Lucina (in charge of childbirth).

Mysterium Cosmographicum
Artichoke, coffee, lilac, musk
Dioptrical Glass
Universe as Mathematical and Boundless.

Longitude Harrison
Prima naturalia
Reviver of Epicureanism
The corpuscularian hypothesis
Insensible perspiration.

Vegetable drugs
Corpses breed worms
Dirt breeds vermin
Sour wine breeds vinegar eels.


# INFUSORIA


Autocrat of the Breakfast Table
Lateral toes of the pig
The ape is a degraded man, the ass, a degraded horse.

## MAN'S PLACE IN NATURE

A hair in the balance-wheel, a little rust on a pinion, a bend in the tooth of the escapement, a something so slight.

Is mother-love vile because a hen shows it?

One-half the size of nature
A to b glabello-occipital line
Detached milk molars
A human superior incisor tooth.


"I possess two vertebrae, a first and last dorsal."


On the Crania of the Most Ancient Race of Man
Both thigh-bones perfect
Man's place in nature
the Human Side of Science.

## DELLA LENA'S POWDER OF MARS

A world bristling with question marks
A horse-hair put in rainwater and left in the sun
Cutting up monkeys, tackled pigs
Healing by second intention
Europe was a cesspool that reeked with contagion.

The training of God's fingers across the sky
Can anything good come out of that rat-eating country?
He wanted Life in the Raw.

"One must read the book of Nature and wander over her Leaves"
as birds their trackless ways
Fabrica, the crime of honest thought
"Wife," said John Kepler, "we are going to Prague"
Fortuitous concourse of atoms
A vile, prophesying almanac
My restless brain goes grinding on—
a "grinding" brain is bad company
The State? I am the State.

They were beaten or strangled with cold water and dosed with drugs
Mustard plasters and Spanish fly were also used
Yeast water, strained, sweetened with sugar, enriched with carbonate of
chalk.

"Facts, facts, I must have proof"
Besides spasmodic events, such as sneezing,
coughing, etcetera
Many of the ordinary acts of life.

# MERE MORTALS

*How heavy was*
*the midnight of woe*
*under the lash of the driver*
*animated by the living spirit of freedom*
*scenes of pollution and blood*
*He is a man-stealer.*

A weird half-sister generally the result of heredity, combined with abnormal education in early youth.

The clouts and buffets of this wicked world still it conveys an unwarranted implication of imbecility.

Drink, guzzle, and syphilis. Could this have been the same as the pretty girl who landed, eager, seasick, and ready for chicken pox? In 1910 his remains were dug up and his thin, light skull was found with its remnants of hair still plastered.

If she had had sense enough to come in out of the wet.

# Rx

## *LORICA*

*Dreams are froth*

Return home by a clean route, going both ways in silence.
Lie face upward toward the hot/sun.
Flying venoms; evil nines; the elf-shot.
Sing this charm nine times into the ear:
Sing frequently into the wounds, and smear with spittle.
Your own image cut in iron or steel, protects against the enemy.

## *ANIMALCULA*

*Man was borne to conquor*
*Man can hit back*

Defend head with hair, and eyes, forehead, tongue, teeth and nostrils,
neck and backside, veins, thighs, intestinal fat, and two hands to my
cranium with hairs on top, a helmut of safety to my head.

## LEECHDOMS

*The little doors of the veins*

*charm. O clear eye, O double clear eye, O eye of clear sight! O darkened eye, O doubly darkened eye, O eye of darkened sight! O eye of sleepy (?), O failing eyes, O painful eyes, like the slaughter of a sheep... like hay (?), like a cup of sour wine, thrown away.*

Take a very fat puppy and skin him, then take the juice of wild cucumber, fat of a vulture, fox, and bear, equal parts, and stuff the puppy therewith.  Then boil him: add wax to the grease that floats on the surface and make an ointment.  Or, if you like, take a frog when neither sun nor moon is shining, cut off its hind legs:  apply the right leg to the right foot, and the left leg to the left foot, and without doubt, you will be healed.

## MAGIC BLASTS

*Up I go, over thee I step*

Sea horse pizel
Scurf
Scammony
Bone of stag's heart + red roses
Sneezing in a hot malady
Three adverbial pills: quick, far, and late.

## THE OLD SNAKE STORY

*The average man looks for something beyond*

Some people think that fish is a brain food and that a mackerel will convert a moron into an Einstein.

*Some people believe that warts can be removed by tying knots in a string and burying the string at a crossroads, in the moonlight*

I have seen a multimillionaire seriously expectorate into his palm and splatter the saliva far and wide at the passing of a white horse.

*Some people believe that if you drink from a garden hose, you may get a snake in your interior*

Hard cheese and celery should be thoroughly chewed.

*Some people believe that if you break out with pimples or boils, it's just the meanness erupting*

A live piscatory specimen in one's stomach is not an enjoyable companion.

*Some people believe that poker players try to improve their luck by rubbing the hump of a hunchback*

Without phosphorous, there is no thought.

*Lots of people think that it is possible to take the eye out, wash it, and put it back*

An X-Ray examination finally showed that she had swallowed an octopus egg, which had hatched inside her anatomy.

# A SHORT HISTORY OF DISCOVERY

# DAUGHTERS OF GENIUS

*A Series of Sketches*


Character of her father - His firmness and decision - Her hospitality - Banquet for two thousand Belgians - The apostle of gentle methods - Her ascension to the throne - Furniture and utensils - She studies Virgil - Her loaf of bread - His dinner song - Mrs. Arnold feigns innocence - Her charitable labours - She dies of overwork - Routine at the palace - Her removal to the Boston Blind Asylum - Incident of the handkerchief - An incongruous couple - Some offensive passages - He makes her a telescope - First tastes of absinthe - Her brutal father - She makes the punch - The Wild Irish Girl - She abolishes torture - Her wonderful beauty - The young widow carried off - A cheap dressing gown - Resumes her man's dress - She revokes her recantation - Burned at the stake - Begins to write - Discovery of her secret - She despises her country - Napoleon refuses to recognize her - Betsy reproved by her father - His will - Her residence in Europe - Convent life - Specimens of her poetry - Her political principals - The closing of her life -

## Medium & Daybreak

A lady is smarter than a gentleman - maybe
A man so various that he seems to be
A million million spermatozoa
A pretty sneaking knave I know.

One window bird sat mourning for her love
Accept thou shrine
Declared that Arab lady
I am a kind of farthing dip.

Ask no more where Jove bestows
Candles, Clerk Saunders, and Mary Margaret,
Daughter of Time, the hypocritic days
Fear not, o maidens shivering.

O little self icicles hung upon the wall
Monarch of her Realm,
Muse of sighs, not moon,
But her Pig – that Pig!

**KIMBERLY ROSENFIELD, WE'VE BEEN LOOKING FOR YOU!**
We are bleeding arterially... Girlhood
Mrs. L.M. Monmouth and how she lived on 40 dollars a year.

WOMEN ECCENTRIC & PECULIAR:

Victory through the tunnel - you call it womb -
The want of furniture - the children neglected -
Makes a man of him - his opinion of her - reforms the household - his
gratitude to her -
Her opinion of him - her grave...

THE MILK DISEASE:

Green boards
She was given to vicissitudes
They ate steak off copper plates.

She was an invalid until she met RB
Shoes sewn from flannel strips - corn meal - oat meal - salt pork -
molasses
Dome parties at Vassar - a pretty sitting room
Chiefest symptoms died away - different from the political
The Tempter takes
Flung-back frock coat - and people like me may well
ask themselves
His wife died young
Deeper shade - lively liberalism.

## The Wandering Uterus

"and now, O woman, we call upon thee to help thyself"

Miss Wiggles is a *sensitive*
large quantity of limpid urine
the most abundant crop of fruit
heavily disguised as venereal passion
noises in the head, glowing balls of light.


Insufflation.


Slow interrupted breathing, turgid neck, flushed cheek.


Proverbially erotic, egotistical, and religious
nasal feeding
charnel house smell.


Dreaming, ETC.
Waking and Sleeping, ETC.
Spectral Lights, ETC.

## Nine Men's Morris

Return of the mad keeper's carriage
Exquisite, musical, and dim prophesies
Moral thumbscrews
falling in studied negligence
Schools of Air.

The lame, the blind, the halt, the warped in intellect
Epileptic, cataleptic, or unbalanced
What is sauce for the goose
Chalice
Live eels, water lobster, sea water, and star-fish.

A darkened room
The law and how you break it.

Say "ouch" "help" and "fire" many times.
Pretend being donkeys and repeat "Heehaw."

(Looking at your feet through the wrong end of the opera glasses).

## *The Girl in Question*

Who died last spring?

    (looking forward to)

Miss Bailey
Mrs. Dyer, the baby farmer
Poor girl's downfall
Cruel, cruel baby farms.

### The Girl Reserve (Number Five)

Missed Paradise by that much
A troop of snowy does
Lady, *viva voce*
Angelica *tete-a-tete*
(Father an invalid and cranky).

*I haven't been so fond of everybody*
*and so pleased with the world*
*since I was a girl.*

Turning in, Lidding up
False Teeth
Core Making in the Foundry.

"Has a wave they come miles to get"
Trashy stuff.

Professor G. Stanley Hall likens this period for a girl.

I Confess
Breezy Stories
Cupid's Diary.

The hyo-glossus, a secret from Rome.

Basting sleeve buckram
Felling edge tape
French felling of collars
Felling collars in the neck
Nose adjuster
The woman who does not live at home
Girl of the Limberlost.

There was emotion far out among the links.

# TRAVELS WITH A DONKEY

*A SOCIAL HISTORY*

BEGINNINGS

Luminary of the system of pleasure
Toddler's tea time in Noah's Ark
Fog, frost, and thaw
Foot clothes of velvet for horses
Petrarch's inkstand
Ozonated sun lounges.

*"Hail then, purveyor of shrimps"*
Almost indecency united in a joint and individual purpose
"Forth to fresh fields and pastures new"
Directions relating to the Manner and Expense of Traveling from
one Place and Country to another.

Green sickness virgins
Unfruitful or miscarrying wives
Alchemists, Dutchmen, Germans, Jews
at the end of a rope on a Swiss glacier
Men hopped in sacks, trundled wheelbarrows blindfold, chased
a pig with a soaped tail.

# THE WEATHER (SCIENTIFIC)

Classes are of two kinds; those which are members of themselves and those which are not. Instances of classes which are members of themselves are the class of non humans, since the class of non humans is itself; and the class of classes which are not members of themselves (since the class of classes is itself a class) are the class of matchboxes and beetles in their cases (in these classes of class). Is the class of all classes a member of itself or not a member of itself?

Detect fallacies, if any, in the following:

Therefore, the longer a man is at the front, the less likely he is to be killed.

Grasp a stick about five foot long behind the back, place a pin on the right hand edge of the seat of a chair, with the palms of the hands facing forwards. Pass stick over head, sit down without touching the floor. Lift right leg and put it round the right arm and through the stick. Without changing your grip, pass the left hand over the head and back and step out of stick, crawl round the back of the chair and remove pin with teeth.

## TRAVELS WITH A DONKEY

Worst vagaries of the climate.

A green Christmas makes a full churchyard.

The Tent is the primary safeguard of the person.

Remember, that without a mattress, you need as many under as over you.

The moon is of no assistance whatever.

Stumpy Jenny Wren
Polly Wash Dish
Gowk
The Yaffle.

A clowder of cats
A seulk of foxes
A richesse of martens
A fesynes of ferrets
A dopping of sheldrakes
A murmuration of starlings.

Use tinned foods, but disguise them.


A Zabaglione boiled is a Zabaglione spoiled.


(Travels with a donkey cont'd)


Mother Sauce


*Don't* cook and attempt to eat young
bracken shoots because the Japanese do.

## EPISODE OF DECAY

She lifts up her crutch
and knocked out their brains
Question: who rang the bell?

Hanging now harms my aunt
Whew!
Rinsed like something sacrificial.

The blighters
Spitting lips once sanctified
She made her breakfast on an edge of his
Maimed and set at naught.

Skin of owls
Venom of unhappy distances
He died of wheaten bread
juicy salads fail'd him.

Shadow pledge
Mr. Mischief branch
Keened damp tissue
by bier side
Icy urn
for her surcharge'd heart
Eyeglass in Gaza.

Space, the bouncer of solitude
EPISTAXIS
SYNCOPE
PERIPALPEBRAL ECCHYMOSIS
"Yes" and "No":

"Am I a Man?" "Am I a Myth?" "Am I a Foreigner?"

Dumb show
Of trespass to land
Of beaches to railways
Of bathing
Of treasure troves to other lost property.

# THE EXCURSIONIST

A peep into futurity
Wither in the virgin thorn
Bleeding for our country
Academy of compliments:

How      do      you      sweat?

He who is only noseless himself
Naked savages and Juan Fernandez
Biscay swells and the mariner
Light, electric, Turkish, Russian, radiant, and other.

Organized Amble
A pleasant walk along the Coast
Balneomania
For the benefit of a person who has a mind.

## THE TABLE-BOOK

A russeton apple has its beauty as well as a peach
Pre-amble on the Kettle-drums
The vox-humane, the cremona or violin-stop,
The double cartel or bass-flute.

"Herrings, herrings, stinking herrings!"
Rat-skin robes for the ladies
Rat pie would be as good as rook pie
A kind of celestial hedgehog
A lover of a chirruping cup.

The simple annals of the poor
for ornament or use
Roasting his wife on a grid-iron
He ogled every mop-squeezer in town
O Tempora!  O Mores!

Marbles, pebbles, etc. he made up into paste
Autobiography of a stone-eater
Before I was borne, my mother dreamed I was an ostrich
I nibbled at every pan and mug
I am promised, by a friend, a shirt of the famous Asbestos.

# DISSERTATIONS ON DOOMSDAY

Via dial-up line?
I'd like it in the following format:

"I'm A Going!"

1 drink; 2 draw; 3 fill; 4 cry "Hy-Jinks"; 5 count just; 6 choose your double
man
"Fleboto-maria"
Quality oranges, quality lemons, holiday limes.

"FOR THE NONCE"
A voider for the nonce
Floralian festival
Misspenders of time and abusers of the creature
Easter-Box
"Isabella-colour"
The fishery is a great nursery
The King's Ostrich.

Koonbees
Unleavened of the flour of Bajeree or Juwaree.

County little known
They are called wild roses,
honey-bees, humble-bees, and wasps
On the west coast of Sumatra
The dial of Ahaz
The united brightness of a fixed number of stars.

HAVE YOU A FRIEND?
TRUE GENEROSITY IS DELICATELY MINDED
Fens, bogs, dens, and caves of death
Up and be doing
Shun will-mongering

Lick honey from off a thorn
Earth bathing


Stockjobber to the lies of the day
The monopolizers to the hopes
of a wet and bad harvest
Secret, black, and baleful workings.


A maddog is none of my bugbears.

# EXCELSIOR REFLECTOR

*Designs in Poetry for a Fashion Spring Forecast*
*(Post-Valentine's Day Massacre)*

STORY OF A DRESS:

Super/ revealing
violently/ form-fitting
asymmetrical cutaway gown.

In this dress/ I felt like/ a woman.

You have to/ stand up straight/
throw out/ your shoulders
and lean/ into the dress.

You have to/ hold your champagne
glass/ a certain way.

You don't need/ a bra
the dress/ holds it/
all together/ for you.

Pressed crepe underwear options
(Brown being the new black)
(Red being the new neutral).

Backless, strapless
sheer net bra
slash-front
bust-boosting bodyslips.

Cotton briefs are like meeting in the rain forest

no longer just for girls being killed going to school
An American Classic
The future never looked so
re-affirming.


Please hear this as pure fashion information
direct from the runways, as the designers intended:

Not all voices/ in fashion/ are calling/ us back
Consider the centrality of macro ruffles
to a woman's spring existence.


Runway looks are all about_____
It is a _____ season in NYC, full of _____
and _____ and in keeping with that mood the big news
is peaches for breakfast, then golf, then a swim!

Be a Pavlova and nothing else!

Kohl-rimmed eyes and a total lack of discretion
Handsome faces half-hidden in the shadows of the night.
The frayed places on your pink kimona.

   *[Musical Interlude]*

   (Sung in a small voice)

      Buy yourself a white dress
      with a lovely sash,
      an ashes of roses sash,
      as pale and crystalline
      as a Greek Ocean—
      and buy yourself
      a leg horn hat—and you will be
      as picturesque as a summer path
      over the mead-ow.

This inner settlement feels like
unhappiness, sluggish apathy,
and hopeless, helpless boredom.


## CAN'T "MAKE IT" WITH YOUR PARENTS?


Pervasive self-dislike follows her here
"I was still a little girl,
I was getting breasts, you know"


## VERY DOWN WHEN YOU WAKENED THIS MORNING?


## ARE YOU FEELING, PERHAPS, THAT YOU'RE A <u>NO GOOD</u> PERSON?


The unwitting burlesque of base female crime
An ever ready & waiting Xerox machine
My own Blueprint for Heaven.


Loving your shame, she breathed deeply
He felt some shame in surveying the unclad women.

Take the lid off/ your relationship/ potential
When I learned to/ enjoy the/ raw feelings of/ your body.


Child adrift in the world herself
Novel hormonal status, household of spells
MGM spectacular
You know, something to do with her own life

*41*

Being me-for-them at the end of a yo-yo.

Ask yourself what they all have in common,
and, you see, they know the following:

You get/ the cold shoulder
if you're not/ wearing a gown.


Shoes cobbled over so thickly
Hose hanging over his hoggers
Miserable mittens made of old rags
Fingers worn out and filth clotted on them
A clouted coat cut short to the knee.

3 yards of purple shamlet
A bonnet of deep murray
A hose of yellow kersey
Laces of silk
Mink cuffs.


The first woman to be a man of letters


[Sex is a red-blooded thing—
 into it she dumped her paint pots]

STEP OUT A BIT WITH A SNAPPY GIGOLO
OR A NEIGHBOR WHOSE WIFE DOESN'T UNDERSTAND HIM.

Having to do with being an individual's
individual creation.

No G-strings, NUDE!

_____wears a gown
of rich brown taffeta
lined with shimmering golden lamé.

From her shoulders extends a curve
of soft, silky velvet
perfectly complimented by a three-tiered tiara.

Golden embroidery and sparkling sequins
swirl together elegantly
at the foot of her gown
and her blonde hair is swept up in curls.


WHAT DO THEY THINK WE DO ON BOY'S NIGHT OUT?


Beauty provides grounding in getting a life
for those of us not blessed in the cradle
Spurred by guilt or excess
stuffed full of celebrity food
ravaged by expensive alcohol
Please!  Cover that mirror!


A Memorandum to Self:

(you are what you think you are)


[A SMALL FASHION SHOW]

The Minimalist

Injects spare style
with a touch of the avant-garde
Safeguards against sheerness.

The Spiritualist

Wears a spectrum of sophisticated
yet earthy tones
first-passage outfits.

The Orientalist

Adds a bit of fantasy to the familiar.

The Prince of the City

Creates pieces
exclusively geared
toward the urban
and the urbane.

The Soft Touch

Delivers a subdued
feminine
super-sexy design.

The Wild One

Our latest bad-boy
and new Head of the House
adds punk to feminine pink
and how-low-can-you-go hipster

The Dissident

Weights the burgeoning trend
with serious glamour
No more icons—it's over.

The Purist

Long favors luxe over no-nonsense
Cool understatements of second skin
Takes you where the Modern is.

The Mix Masters

Demonstrate flair for vintage hodge-podge
and making-out in fields of raspberries
Mastercast declarations.

The Explorer

Goes on safari
Inspiring the traditional
accented with tribal themes
How shall the garment be judged?

The Romantic Lead

Offers sexy slips
Drape-necked tigers
with an edge.




Our instincts said no, but fashion prevailed.


The debacle of a bare leg in winter
Back to peddling that old corporate standby
It was as bad as it gets
"Lose the shoe"
Slag off my tiara

a custom-made caprice
against suntanned skin.

CHECKLIST:

-How to get the Look Of The Moment-

It's going to take more than a summer's psychological load.

You in that little black dress—
it's YOU he wants to unwrap!

This is a little tale that could lead us
anywhere:

3 Poiret dresses at a roadside barn sale,
A bundle of beading,
A Greek toga cannibalizing itself,
The private showrooms
of a handful of specialists.

*I would be very sorry to see*
*spilled wine on a '47 Dior.*

Romantic, but with an edge,
like a girl who's been about.

The "American Look."

Illustrated by both
naturalness in manner
and make-up.

The friendly smile
the confident, unaffected air,

with head up.

She has a well-scrubbed look,
she is alive, alert
not submerged
by current fashions or feelings.


SHOW THE WORLD TWO DIFFERENT SIDES OF YOUR
INTERESTING SELF!


If a personality or fashion clinic is available,
have yourself checked in.


Searing pang of shame, social chitchat,
Mellow display of feigned good-fellow-cheerfulness
sometime with blustery lecturing.

Give the lady what she wants
A dress of apricot silk, with train
A sage-green silk street dress
A frock of grenadine moire, a watered silk fabric
Langtry bangs.


A dress of silver-wrought brocade of Parisian
texture combined with point d'Alencon lace
and silver passementerie threaded with tiny pearls
with lace edging and a taffeta skirt and many
gildings and French shirrings.

The new styles are quite classic
The new hats are classic
The new woman will be classic
And the popular girl will be classic also
Your new face will be classic—
Study your face and try to make it a classic.

Tip the Glam-O-Meter!
Look like a nubile mermaid.
Love me, love my retro-naughty!

Fashion is the Esperanto of shape, color, and detail.

"We hope that things will be more poetic,
and that they will somehow turn out in a beautiful way."

News Flash:

A skeleton holding its density.

The dress that lets you run a business from your bathtub.

They just want to dream a little,
to look pretty.

The climate that bred a hot-house creature
(and other reasons to sit in the dark).

Plain ol' vanilla minicollections
Throughout home and office
(A line between passion and aggression)

MISS USA:

"I love crawfish,
and I can peel them myself!"

Her elegant Victorian jacket and green jacquard skirt
are complemented with sumptuous
faux-mink trim and glistering
rhinestone buttons.
An elegant stole and gold braid add a festive touch.

*Clothes are about who you are
not what you're wearing.*


The Rules of Simplicity:
  Courtesy
  Integrity
  Perseverance
  Self-Control
  Indomitable Spirit
  and No Ruffles!


Humans can bear only so much austerity.

Simple Is In and Labels Are Out.

Undecorated luxury is unassailable.

I'm not saying that a baby is an accessory
but with it you take along your sense of style.

Next
everyone will leave
some stained green chairs
and a tight discriminating stitch.

A picture of you
at the side of the grave
the still-narrow bed and
all your teeth are there—
not shed,
not entwined,
just tired.

[The middle of winter
is a rough time
for the restless.]

# SARAFEM

*My analyst says love is homesickness*


The Greeks had a word for it
the word begins with 'H'
That tinkly music they play
in my aromatherapy clinic.

Milk is always in fashion
It's the *world* of Calvin.

You walk beneath angels
in the vaulted ceilings
and think for a minute about your own
tucked in bed at home.

Women are trained in this culture
to do things for others
and therefore feel guilty
spending on themselves.


Try-on-a-thon.

The It Slit.

Let your shameless armpits run naked through the streets.

Worldwide vacation for 18-35 year olds.

In a sense, women of our generation
are at a crossroads.

You . . . you're the one . . . you are the only reason.

Shoppers shame and self-loathing
I dropped my credit cards in a jar
and stored them in the freezer.

If your parents didn't love you enough
there's not enough Versace in the world
to fill that hole.

The three C's — credit card, cash, and check.

Put Miss Havisham on the back of a motorcycle
and you've got my point of reference.

Be Everyone You Are.

I love my scar.

Isn't doing laundry therapeutic?


Monotony cloaked with ideology
Swims softly in the moth proof trunk
A great playground for
an unforced style of living
where progressive couples find romance
and antiauthoritarian children romp around.

Battling members of communes sink from view
Somebody opens a center
just to study his disease
Clean, dry vanity
In the great ocean of life's moods
Where everything that is fine and beautiful in this world
is for sale
Vienna is as close as Malibu.

Everyone who crosses this path
regards this amalgam as the elixir of life
*It is so...21st Century*
Everyone is supposed to make his or her own poem out of it.

Waking up is like politics
Is it the inner clock?

We, the really nice people, of the United States of America
We, the people,
of the Emporio Armani Exchange.


Our volunteerism?  We will offer you the best products of our care, the
most self-effacing and most agreeable to use.  For all this, your avarice is
indispensable.  Don't hesitate to make yourself part of all that you
remark upon.  The incontestable efficacy of products with incessant ame-
lioration grace the contact with you.  Associate with our technological
research of the avant-garde.

If you have a particularly esthetic smile, we will respond to you personal-
ly.  Our professionals were acquitted with incomparable experience to
vacate your beauty problems.  They are there for you to understand
them, for you to console them, and for you to help them become more
beautiful,  more clashing, more long time.  IF YOU KNOW...

I.

If you know the enthusiasm, the dynamism we put into all we offer you
with our millions of products of beauty,  you will know how to remain
beautiful longer.  THE LOVE OF BEAUTY...

II.

If you know...Poor nothing isn't too handsome for your beauty.  Our
Laboratories of Research select the activities the most precious, the most

efficacious, the most sure.  THE EFFICACY OF BEAUTY...
III.

If you know...For your beauty and for respect of Nature privilege always
the plants dangerous to test.  ECOLOGICAL BEAUTY....

IV.

If you know,  you will never have to face your beauty problems.  We are
true professionals, in permanence to your listening.  Tell us what preoc-
cupies you.  THE LISTENING OF BEAUTY...

V.

If you know... Leader in Europe.  High games.  Counts of millions of
women of fidelity.  But for us, each one of them is unique.  Write us, let
us judge you.  THE FIDELITY OF BEAUTY...


We listen, and we counsel.


Our honesty.  For all this we are indispensable.  Don't hesitate to part
with your remarks.


Out of purity and equilibrium is borne this primordial beauty act.  A
crash of lightening brings clattering youth to your skin.


Your chauffeur will remove your makeup with the palm of his hand and
will bring a temperature to your skin.  With all the surface of his hands,
he will make simple contact,  without pushing.

Repeat this jest 5 or 6 times.  Try to prove or effect one "selling" who aspires to impurity without irritating or displacing tissue.

## WISDOM FROST

Etch a moment in platinum
and it will live forever.
It's how you make happiness immortal
and how you make a moment a milestone.

No other man-eater is special enough
to mean forever.

*I like you; let's go out and do it all*

Cadillac whiteness
Reflective and impermeable
Who will you be in the next 24 hours?

*Stones of the first water*

A tip:

Have the porter at your hotel call and add you to the VIP list.

The scent of kingship has a blue blood breeding of its own. Known only
to the high borne and the highly visible.

Anyone whose been awake for the past six months knows that in metal,
the color of the moment is yellow.

Q: Is being borne into wealth a burden?

Well, maybe not the stuck-tamponless-with-Afghan-rebels part.


Knock back a few over peanuts and patter.
Boost your self esteem with a Bic
(Deceit can be very freeing)


From ME to shining ME.



Have theft detection devices embedded which will be
deactivated at the register or service desk

*Water take this fever from me*
*Carry it from here far out to sea*

Take the stockings you've worn during the day
Cross the legs to form an X

Turn out the lights before you undress
change into a black nightgown and quietly slip into bed

Go to an oak tree on a chilly autumn day
put your catch in a bureau drawer at home and say:

*Summer dress, let me not feel winter's storm*
*Through chill and wind keep me safe and warm*


Will my husband receive a promotion?


Fad Kingdom, if space
cuz all you guys sap code all ughs

mad, mad kings.
A 401K for the body
Press Link information exchanged in your skin
to help sustain its livelihood.


*You're on earth, there's no cure for that*


*Just after the war, I'm wearing a dress*
*sent from relatives in America*

Beyond beige
Over olive
What does khaki mean *now?*

Stand atop a figurative tower
in the Central Square
of the imaginary
City of Fashion.

A Japanese-made little flight attendent-esque scarflette

I don't have much of a waist
This will give me a waist.

Prada Citizen!
Vote the party line
The Slim Skirt party.

This isn't brain surgery
it's a skirt.


Exposing scanties sagacious ladies at the girdle shop
"Ironic prep"
Preppino

Haven't designers checked the Dow?
*It was like talking to a shrink who really understands hair*


How your Skin is affected by Life


Late night scenes covered in blood
with a prosthetic wand on your face.


Green is a dangerous color, even in the best of times.


With your head on someone's shoulder
you hear each  fiber in the cloth.


A place more colorful awaits you
Fashion without an expiration date
Friends well past their expiration dates
A beauty futurologist
Out multitask Jennifer Lopez
For a playing-in -the-wind glow
The curiosity that mixed race beauty triggers.


Fashionation

Hydration is a measure of issues of nature.  First exposed to world
exteriors.  She surmises heat and cold, wind and TV.   Climatized.
Other factors which give thirst:

Grace + 2 plant extracts which have the capacity to regulate their needs
in  hostile and oppositional milieu.

The Penis Lambada, a very dry tree, stacked with water and necessities for evaporation.

The Elongated Himanthalia, Algae of Wesson, have emerged to uncover parts of the sea, reunited in the same formula, these 2 active additions permanently assure and regulate.

Lunelle—Birth control inspired by the moon.

A sultry oasis of feather and palm fronds
Every bit the sugary dewdrop
Cat-suit-clad girl band
A place where the sun always shines
Black uniforms tight as a condom
More Upper than Crusty
When they add you up, what do you spell?

ARE YOU IN A PRETTINESS PANIC?
Lure a tag tucking nape touch.

I travel with them in a sock
Young girls dressed in twin sets
O dear, you don't have a dress watch?

Live what the actors act
Smash your Ferrari into a meat truck.

*We understand, we live here too*

SHA-din-froy-dah

All the grace of a 1902 Cadillac going uphill.
Hear those birds chirping?
they're discussing your bold new coat.

Jump!   It's Argyle Day!


Andy Warhol was always in style.

Respect is not a very creative thing
Wee Wolford fishnets
Supermodel sphincters
Longitude:  Lash Out!
Vita  da  Cashmere
Mall  of  Me.


I WANT TO DENIM THE WORLD!


It's time to storm the white rope
and see how the fashion 1/2 lives
It's a vicarious, voyeuristic ride.  Welcome!


Politics may be backsliding
but fashion forges ahead.


The facelift sensation is immediate
"it tingles" says the patient, bleeding slightly
acticalm retranslates
the chemical message
from the brain
and talks the skin
into being calm.

Hyda Zen
is cheaper
than an actual

therapist.
Be Yourself
It's a very tough act to follow.

The trouble with London
is it's too much fun!
At the end of the day, the girls just love glamour!

I Am Your Child
Father Time has finally met his match
If she had a style prayer to chant every night.

Young girls are tired
of wearing all that junk
Youth is the invention
of middle-aged people.


You've got to get a lining for that
Prophetic dream
They dream of a girl
who likes a big juicy steak
a foaming mug of beer
and a thick hunk of pie.

Luxury is what you don't see
Emotion unabashed by the unique culmination of different elements
400 years of Catholicism
50 years of American Las Vegas.

Give a child
the priceless gift
of summertime fun & hope.


India, in a pop way.

# VERBALI
*(projective-identification translations from the Italian)*

## WHEN INTERPRETATIONS FAIL

Symptomatic outcroppings
Residue of childhood
Islands of authority
The priest is in and
about the meaning these monuments have for us
Join us in loving it

A dead elm flowers in winter as the saint's remains pass
Spirited and witty in the Gothic style
Sit on your cathedra
The angel announces sacrament of initiation/
dispute with doctors
1/3 over burial-hope-faith-justice-prudence-fortitude-charity-temperance

Who is the "Flower" in question?
Sheep-herding, music, wine-making, metallurgy, astrology, building,
medicine, weaving
Travelling protagonists
(This is the tutty
here is the spodium)

Value of a Venetian silver groat
River's gold dust
Pepper, nutmeg, spikenard, galangol
Vitamin's way
No gas guiliani
Jazz pistachios

Are "Heart" and "Earth" spelled the same?

# PRATTLE VICINITY

O nelly! Exotic oasis for flower, fruit, cortex, paper, radish, resin, cherry gas and lore of besotted fantasy

::::::::::::

All the rivets of this mouth and nary a bottle to drink. Singular note estate of maximum sapiens composed bouquets. In order to spend memory or sweep up a fantasy, vague and song-like not better perceptions of reality. For calming passions and exciting the senses, to follow the "I" most segregated and closed in a puff of misery

::::::::::::

Take calmly the hand. A miserable gesture, sweetness. Impart a mongrel without cure. The moment in leather is coming. Perfume begins to modify you slowly, taking every precaution. Potatoes conserve around the year. Record and reheat well each bottle of color and light. This most simple system for maintaining in the long run is inalterably your fragrance and that of the proletariat—a vapor without gas, preserving external aggression

::::::::::::

Scope out the multiplicity of a swelling nature. The initial centurion of which she cut involuntarily the "notes of the head." Schemes volatile and of little duration. Half-simple are constitutions, like sugar (lemon, bergamot, mandarin) of the labiate salves (eye-coverings): (rosemary, hyssop, mint)

::::::::::::

Travel with the dominant one o "notes of quality." Pack something minute after discovering your own "notes of the head." This lore is definitely the personality of your spouse, sentry in red, artichoke, jasmine, and windmill

::::::::::::

In order to finish the "notes of the found" from this intense aroma, search for the single note from the soul: Patchouly, Labrador, Musk of What Will Be, Benzocaine, Incense

Separate out the sensibilities of your every day arc: a game without nuance from the caves of erasure and pinocchio. Between senility and dieting. The ears naturally make a refined gesture: perfume each inductee under the collar and follow with a polka. This profundity will eventually evaporate and create a harmonium

### The Acquiring of Frisky

Polite, fragrant like a room of bathtubs. Generous for guessing later security and vitality

In quest of a found toilet, fresh and amorous or a fantastic wood ideal for a reunion of disgruntled flour-children. A mediterranean car after the rains, full of grassy distaste

### Vetiver for the Reunion

Fruits of a gloppy recipe that provokes the contras from far away with their masculine and exquisite equilibriums. Only for aristocrats, a quasi-sensation of Asia

### Imperial-Waters

Political freshness from the essence of antique sapiens. No dossier needed for this unique colonial slant

A bouquet thrown into hyperspace on the arm of a fresh brigade. The
High Alps at noon
Lent, if Spain lives
Ideals for glide-sports;  accompany yourself in a young body dynamic
and in top-form

Assorted miseries of all occasions.  No one is excluded.  For some, the culmination of fulfilling absolute fidelities

Emotional, meditative, intense, borne of man.  Full of women's characteristic impetuousness and ardency.  Like a respite on scorched palm fronds fresh from a secular holiday

A record of morning, sentiments rise from the country-side.  Primordial breezes full of youth's ammonia and optimism.  Irresistible, like a filter for love

Ravaged in the fire, small grains of pepper-seduction-sauce.  For this ass a fortress of emotion, conquest, and victory.  Same for the intense but silent voice squabbling for generous romantic love

Ravaged femmi-cile.  Like night-music, vibrant with insistent recordings

Medieval ingenuous, held by the muzzle in stressy times.  Exclusively long-lasting planks of charm.  Inanimate apparitions of personalized women who scorched when they spoke

Old with the cruelty of lavender.  Symbol of esoteric prizes and spiritual after-ski altruism; optimism rentals.   A soiled note that can't be revived

A flowing idiot arrives without embracing the recession. Flies to Curacao without suggestions, reprimands, or incantations

*69*

Over the breezy, unimaginative grunge
of base security quizzes, there
is rarely a passing of trapped
radar through the fields,
branches, and ventilation systems

From a sepia-tint of the vatican
to a lost son of mercy, short
on space from which to search the soul, mothers are
called to re-group then deposited without
learning the 4 variations of seduction:
fascination, fascism [Indoor Music]


                    Each one of us is in an animal state
                    and also one of illusion where charm
                         becomes irreversible.  Lone fire
                              payola by credit card




                    Your fascinating ramparts/ imperatives.
                    Gas up each extract, you daring
                                Sensation
                         A crescendo in your personality

# LE TEMPS REVIENT

Is your life . . .


*Sensual and Passionate? (Tubes without guardians)

*Dynamic and Bubbly? (Pepper of your days)

*Calm and Irradiated? (Keep a distance)

*Fascinating and Seductress? (Your humours will melt with flower-fire)

*Holding and Songstress? (Make an internal game with gliding according to exquisiteness)


> *Set down in my books as a debtor/*
> *master of the country*
> *outbursts of psychopathic inhumanity*
> *ribbons and sugared nuts*
> *dancing to the music of lutes*
> *Nine Fools Are Out*

I'm a small person of very little consequence

<>

My envy of others is great, yet I do
nothing to better my position, despite
knowing I could achieve all they have
achieved.  I used to expect things to be
handed to me without working for them, and
I've come to know that is not how
one betters oneself, but still I have
a little hope that I will advance without
any exertions on my part.  I've already
passed the age I'd determined for myself
that I'd have been a Somebody, but
still cling to an idea that I'll be
given my opportunity, even though I
have nothing to show for it at an advanced age.
I don't know what I want in my life, but still feel I
should be given a spotlight to showcase
my very hidden talents


Banishments are commonplace punishments
Dirty dungeon at the bottom of a town
A disorderly gaggle of uncles
Wine and wax

(He had been known
on summer days
to strip the rich clothes
from his dirty body
and roll around
naked in his garden)


Temperance-Prudence-Fortitude

Mild measures are useless
Alters splashed with blood and wine
Built in safe-hair

## ZOOLOGIA

To be rich and have an appointment is
time to count conditions
Meteorological stations
that can possibly anticipate or postpone the flowering of the Azalea

Closings for festivals of infrastructure
The bitter seductions of Paleontology
An infinite dilation of the Baptistry
(according to old sources)
(traditional Heaven and Hell)

The risen bagel being an instrument of passion
The illusion of cabinets half-open
Please break your visit to the church


The scent of the iris (the Florentine "lily"), symbol of the gentle Tuscan
landscape, is perceptive as something mysterious in Chianti wine and as
something romantic in the face-powder of beautiful women in crinolines


Grand fire of the masculine world
The Duchess of York in her needy infancy
Girls on the Jelly
Touch of (d)Evil
The light in you, Giotto superstar


(Well, there's a hard minute between prosthetic breastfeeding and the
girl from Santa Croce)

Florenz smells of Iris (how nice).  Even when she is a small girl and quite
gray there will be conflicts.  (Good Girl)  (come here)
what's that?
property rights
more baby—more toast
show your mind-set
pulling—wagons

She was this way and that.  This was the way she was wanting to be.  She
was that way when she wasn't being like this but that was a very hard way
to be.  She was being very hard in that her little girl made her mad.  She
had to be up all night and be a little mad at this girl whom she made that
way

# PROJECT-DOMUS

Recuperate krylon cocoa
Recipe brindled aromatics
Predisposed to sensorial schedules daily kaka
Diffusion of disgust
Creation of a network for each agent who participates
in rotting cocoa (pleading of tasting).

The marriage must be celebrated. I unite 1/2 oleo with the Noble Old!
The Noble World!

Let me lead you to the base of the brain of the cocoa. Distilled 100% in
mother-bath and limbic ram. Each time a stoppered bottle comes to
penetrate the plantagenates of cocoa, from that thing in the memory, to
a time when the earth will be perfumed with cocoa.

## The Cult of Cocoa

The cult of Cocoa signifies a belief in gusto and
1) Information of consumerism
2) Conservation of our biodiversity


DON'T SLEEP but combat the logic of the marketplace which has pro-
duced a uniform taste and almost extinction of cocoa. DON'T SLEEP
but rise up from the forest and press on the art of respect and
patrimonial genetics of each variety borne on an ecosystem complete
and delicate. The noble and oily seeds of the Ancient and New Worlds.

DON'T SLEEP but be a protagonist in this romance of the "knight of
cocoa"

DON'T SLEEP—bear the logo of cocoa—the rose of cocoa—the
corsair flag, all integral ambiance. The forested heritage raining
commercialized national genes

76

DON'T SLEEP but be recognized throughout the world for cruel originality

92% of the harvest of the world will be less pregnant (a bottom taste of razzmatazz and astringency, a grade of superior fermentation)

In this great centennial year, cocoa lives in a salvaged state, declining the best from a vital circle. Interdependent, needing the shade of the banana tree and humid earth

Give me mud, parrots, and small meatballs which are the favorites of cocoa. Gas, abandoned and gushing from the decomposing fruit of the brain. Safeguards signify the extinction of pocket-space from the hands of men. Durations of tonsillitis materializing in a war in which we can't loose our heads. Undesirable dispersions of viscosity

DON'T SLEEP but be natural and rich like a fruit in season

Why are secondary aromas so important?
Because there exists a certain + correlation between aromatic traits on the one hand and persistent sweetness and roundness on the other

Esmereldas, warm tropical scent.
The freshness of spring foam, the strabismus of Venus, aftertaste of golden tobacco.

Frankness, the synthesis of the 3 balances of elegance thanks to a soft, fine brush stroke
Porcelana-the pearl of elegance, ricotta in its elegance

(Grazie per pensare)



Best Wishes to all you enamourds

Love is an aspect of perfume splendour lacquer
baking soda ocean ferns air song

Venus cleanses and tones people who take by the hand their kisses
Walk through the door of this here night
But people who lead, they are not next
they never will be the people who are next



(The weasel with a branch of rue)



*Victory loves care*
(The oyster opening in the sun)
*Deservedly precious, she came forth from the sky and the sea*

## EXCLUSIVE CLAMOR

Like every year, you risk to create a speculative. One of the major curiosities will be the presence of the subconscious of Luciano Pavorotti (and Caroline of Monaco who milks her son with love)

Another year and the pharmacy becomes indispensible. Panorama of medicine. After having mated a giraffe's head with a woman of the world and three months before the state proclaimed him the sexiest man of the year, this fascinating actor crescendos (contrary to fathers, doting, and steely auto-controlled)

No. A woman with propane in the dreams of her desires emphatically adds acid to the presence of another woman and of a child. The public feminine, a night of underdog love. Napoleon is happy anywhere


What estate becomes a city of the world?

Impaired, strange language, important for your tomorrows
Important to keep you gassed and also experienced
Unforgettable, to bring a dove who has a tongue and speaks to us
A local, international dove, consecrated ragamuffin of 50 Easters
The spy who studies becomes peaceful and also diverting!

*Ciao! I am Anna Belmondo*

*I've scorched myself lugubriously. I've decided to transfer my diverse estate where some company of lice will participate with a vacancy*

*This will be my first time to dive into Easter with sole and put up the suppressed mast of a dossier of diversity—life in England*

*Mothers also have quantities of causes and invest in communes. My family hospital. My best mood to know, my state to all the world. We all stay the same*

*(Anna went helter skelter to a principal course in 20 lessons a day. After each morning lesson, she could be invited to an organized excursion each afternoon)*

*Pay attention to the yellow factions: the part evident with this color is particularly evident: ring at every indication of this symbol*

*Here it is, bridge by bridge, all the particulars of a vacation.*
*Each day, the first lesson is at the breakfast table.*
*Live to possess a selected family consecrated to style and culture of the new country*

Great Time Organizer—never have a minute free!

A costly estate is difficult to salute. Scrambled photos and ballads with the rhythm of a compressed Europe

A lesson of dormant madrigals

Many agencies have tried to imitate the discotech, but few have done it

The ultimate kiss of adornment
The witch and iniquity of right

Medieval and Renaissance essences which obey complete and
insinuating sentiments

Nostalgia of Love of Time
Luscious baths of the women of Ancient Greece
Giaggiolo

For the love of Iris, mother of Florence,
from the city of art, a collection for all your beauty and enthusiasm

Spanish Conquistadors in the rigorous terrains of tropical America

Be Free

Colors and ideas to live in liberty
Be a protagonist in your own life


Suit: the two or three piece uniform worn by office workers.
Tie: a strip of cloth worn round the neck, often colored and shaped
differently


Why wouldn't the others go to the yacht club?
1. survive: get through a crisis
2. dangling: swinging down
3. owners: people to whom things belong
4. yacht: a large pleasure boat, usually without sails
5. threat: a promise to harm someone
6. atmosphere: the feeling in a place
7. cargo: things taken by boat or plane to another place,
usually to be sold

Where do you think the money comes from at the present?


Do you think that people who get into trouble at sea should have to pay for the help they get?  Give your reasons:

8. relieved: happier or feeling better about something
9. victim: the one who suffers


Explain these:

a) Tape:

b) Records:

c) "Send" button:

d) Position

e) Destination

Who said...?

a) Who said "You do it?"

b) Who said "No, YOU do it"

c) Who said "Hello, John"

d) Who whispered?

e) Who said, "We're ready, thanks"

# EUROWARM

I am woman
I am not demented
extravagant, singular, extracted, curious, counter-current, nor of a
volcanic and electric nature

I will continue on this road to master my passions
Fishing for allure, style, and fascism of man
What body do you want?
Marvels have allies


(A proverb recited each night, with every scandal, will ensure 3 days of
marvels)



In this region, in this world of ours, rich in grain and rubbed evidently
with emotion, is truly the marvel of our fugue. With its negative and
positive polarities like a manifesto of all animal states complete and
befogged, resuscitated from memorabilia. That is to say, from the most
beautiful person that can provoke admiration and joy, in a word, blitz


Marvels are not a simple surprise. Nor a co-payment for closure in time.
An alabaster core with something that we cannot visit but evaporates into
quasi-existence. Many volts to treat a funny piston

## SECRETS FOR PEACE:

*Have a nice trip and a fresh mouth*

Your organ of protection

A marvelous surplus of gold, profusion of marmalade, and richness of dice

Whispered: said in a very quiet, breathy voice

Rome to touch
(A NEW GUIDE TO THE CAPITOL)

It is a new mode to describe Rome by her silenced heart.  Her Indian son tripped over her with inattention, in front of the beautiful monuments of the city


Divided city
Take a mental shower every day
Enter a partitioned moral sense of scoop
Lucrative foundations in Switzerland, ambient camp
Give a sum of money, property, or statuary to effect testimonial lashing

## ECHO:

One day exit the house and breathe in the wind via the smog, an aria of cleanliness and of faraway. Because of your memory comes a perfume which rends you lightheaded. Is this the perfume of diesel? Not only to regulate your station but also the interior coldness

I would like to conclude with words more important than me:

# A SELF-GUIDED WALK

INFORMATION FOR THOSE WHO HAVEN'T
BEEN BUT ARE GOING, THOSE WHO
HAVE BEEN AND ARE GOING BACK
AND THOSE WHO DON'T EXPECT TO GO BUT WILL

## First Stop: The City on a Hill

Sit for awhile in your surroundings.  Here is a sanctuary
where people can perceive the grandeur of space
the immensity of the universe

(In a crib on Halloween "in your own little world" someone
 with a Mickey Mouse mask looked through the window
and terrified you)

What kind of place is hell?

Leisure with dignity

The Sun meets her spouse
our little Earth

Audioanimatronic Cro-Magnum figures painting cave-wall animal effigies

In here, Mozart performs his best operas on the harpsichord.

Enter through neo-classical allegorical gates and refreshing canals

*The wearied mind's demand for relief in unconsidered
muscular action*

I know a secret—
would you like to hear it?—
It's the secret of happiness

*91*

## Second Stop: Front Lawn

Don your silver badge and come by boat to float through dark, tree-lined passageways with gardens erupting from thousands of glimmering lamps and polyethylene leaves snapped to trees for immediate shade and foliage.  A gust of wind whips the young lady's skirt around her ears while a clown aims a cattle-prod between the legs of her beau

## Third Stop: Reflecting Pool

Blue animated sperm race at yellow eggs wearing aprons

A life-sized dummy, when punched,
registers the power of that blow

Starshine shoots through a special-effects "starball"

Hordes of bunnies on the dunes

Bones of representatives resting in their cases


How to tell God "I love you"

## Fourth Stop: Cornerstone and Loggia

Gorgeously attired members of the titled class survey your entire world
with one glance

Arising from the dirt strip are shops, a camel, a chunk of Chicago
concrete, Bedouin tents, and a Ferris Wheel

"It's always fun to be free"

Butterflies as pets,
Mother's new electrical servants

Screw-ups are assigned to the brains
of squid, lungfish, Groucho Marx-like toucans


"This chicken doesn't need a brain, he's going into politics"

## Fifth Stop:  The Tower

The silver sheath shines brightly as the sun flares off its facets.
Synthesized Medieval hoe-down.  Special structures which pour forth
smoke and vomit flames.  Jefferson becomes sick of being a prisoner in
the attic.  The making of double nostalgia both French and human:
throw clay balls filled with scented water at 12th century horsemen

A bitter wind whooshes through the speaker system

## Sixth Stop: Gardens

Your feet will be unsuspectingly activated by hidden triggers
A mule trudges round and round beneath the surface of the Earth

(What a time to die, just as I was getting this award)

The smellitzer pumps swamp aroma

Remember, it won't get better until you
get involved

## Seventh Stop: Colonnade

For service and cruelty.
Roses, cherries, and nightingales
carefully cast in Duraflex.
"Perfect pleasure carry us all"

The serpentine is the optimal line of beauty
The skeletal roller coaster
casts the visitor's eyes heavenward.
The man in the jumpsuit walks up to the bears
and offers them bread

Disembark on a moon
complete with prancing moon maidens
distributing green cheese

## Eighth Stop: Displays, Film Center, and Amphitheater

6-Star Chef World
Interior boasts a circle of boxes holding buttered bread.
Go where the rich go
Move around the lagoon in the prow of a longboat.
See a mermaid with nipples
Plunge into a chute
and fall forward into the North Sea

## Ninth Stop: Azalea Garden and Hillside Stream

We offer sunshine that grows bright in the afternoon. Water sweeps away a world—a sudden simulated rainstorm. An actualization of the hymn-book image of heaven, imitation gaslights. Pixie dust that stays on your skin forever. "Will you marry me?" written in chocolate swirls

## Tenth Stop: Visitor's Center

Neal George
Franco George
Pigoff County
Antigua
West Indies

It's certain that in your lifetime, you've bought a lot of greeting cards
A plaster bust of the Mouse with the Human Ear
Tied-up puppet children
Most eccentrics don't wear fright wigs and magenta tights
You will be honored at a picnic on the banks of a river
A moss-covered bunny decorated with silk and dried flowers
in the Germany cart
Bullet-hole-covered getaway cars
If we see a sizzling steak, we conclude that it was just taken from the stove
The joy of playing alone while strangers watch

## Eleventh Stop: The Great Teacher's Kiosk

Wampum, kettle, a blanket,
three pounds of gunpowder, and a diamond-studded police badge
Develop a level of unshakable confidence
Questions for the new millennium:
Do you love your favorite color as much as most people?
What do you most prefer to put ketchup on?

## Twelfth Stop:  Return to the City on a Hill Interior
## (The Way to Live Forever)

Full of distortion mirrors.  Priceless do's and don'ts
This drug has been prescribed especially for you—
don't give it to others

When and where was your first kiss?

Biblical couple, long hair was his strength

Famous mouse couple

Nursery rhyme about a thirsty couple
who stumble and receive a severe head injury

Star-crossed lovers, tragic play, family feud

Reporters for the Daily Planet
often seen in telephone booths and tights

A word to your parents:

We will advise of changes, (if any) when work progresses

## SPECIAL EVENT—in an orange grove—"The Way" issued by Corporate Guest Affairs

Join 4-H, raise chickens, sell eggs!
Creamy concoctions of history to beguile flinty souls.
The bear who steals the honey pot measures up to his opportunity.
A fresh idea a minute spreads bread upon the waters

Remember, it won't get better until you get involved

Will all employees please rise and head east toward the enemy?
It's clean at every turn—green grass and flowers
George Washington gets up from his chair
The water tank leaks all over you on a hot day while robot bison graze

Create a "unique factor" in all you do.
Service without servitude
Maintain a humble mind,
Leave a good trail
*my* food area, *my* dumptruck
*focal* things, *focal* practices

There is little rowdiness
where Lady and the Tramp at their famous spaghetti dinner
Human error is eliminated
A bald customer is used as a prop
A lost children's logbook
Height is an index for age
He is frozen, awaiting appropriate medical developments

## HOSPITALITY HOUSE

Rivers ran dry and there was
a shortage of drinking fountains
Davy Crockett was soaked by sprinklers
A gas leak emptied into the land
Bus drivers were "cast members"
and Utopia meant "no place"


## ENERGY PLANT

Air-conditioning blows the dust away
Efficiency villas built for vacationers
Lowered amounts of water-borne amoebas
A platform collapses during band rehearsal
All persons entering must step in bleach solution
Lava made of styling gel


## EMPLOYEE BENEFITS

Beat their personal best at the turnstiles
Master egg painters, candy sculptors
"She must have loved her parents a great deal"
Canned regional faux folksy accents
inviting us to sing along
Remember, it won't get better until you get involved

## WASTE REMOVAL

The yakoose is a cross between a yak and a moose
One gets kidnapped in each scene
Pineapples are artificially stimulated by ethylene
Dry dog food, chicken pellets, and amino acids mixed with dental plaster
Heat pasteurized sand
Water appears wetter, fire hotter

## TRANSPORTATION

Meteors are projected chocolate chip cookies
Machines and tools are shoddy
Stomping on a human face
More future on the threshold of tomorrow!
Histories we can live with
We sit back, keep our mouths shut

## GLITCHES

A very pouty Mona Lisa ignored
Pioneer families blow on painfully reddened feet
A stagecoach is stopped by a steam-snorting bull
A horse stares at a horseless carriage
You've gotta remind yourself it's the 20th century
What a delight to march and sing along the Freedom Trail!

## LAYOUT AND LANDING

At the entrance is a drunk robot snoring
Fully furnished Fleetwood trailers complete with maid service
The Marshmallow Marsh Excursion ends in a miniature
marshmallow roast
A woman with a cane walking down a cobbled street
Omelets superb avec jambon
On this and every turn, we'll be making progress

## PARADES

Now is the Best Time of Your Life
Rover has become Queenie who becomes Sport
Life is a prize, enjoy every minute
The open snake, the balustrade, the inside corridor,
the inside open snake
Ropes, chains, metal, wood, naugahyde, velvet
Thank you, and have a happy new day

# ROOF BOOKS

- Andrews, Bruce. **EX WHY ZEE**. 112p. $10.95.
- Andrews, Bruce. **Getting Ready To Have Been Frightened**. 116p. $7.50.
- Benson, Steve. **Blue Book**. Copub. with The Figures. 250p. $12.50
- Bernstein, Charles. **Islets/Irritations**. 112p. $9.95.
- Bernstein, Charles (editor). **The Politics of Poetic Form**. 246p. $12.95; cloth $21.95.
- Brossard, Nicole. **Picture Theory**. 188p. $11.95.
- Champion, Miles. **Three Bell Zero**. 72p. $10.95.
- Child, Abigail. **Scatter Matrix**. 79p. $9.95.
- Davies, Alan. **Active 24 Hours**. 100p. $5.
- Davies, Alan. **Signage**. 184p. $11.
- Davies, Alan. **Rave**. 64p. $7.95.
- Day, Jean. **A Young Recruit**. 58p. $6.
- Di Palma, Ray. **Motion of the Cypher**. 112p. $10.95.
- Di Palma, Ray. **Raik**. 100p. $9.95.
- Doris, Stacy. **Kildare**. 104p. $9.95.
- Dreyer, Lynne. **The White Museum**. 80p. $6.
- Edwards, Ken. **Good Science**. 80p. $9.95.
- Eigner, Larry. **Areas Lights Heights**. 182p. $12, $22 (cloth).
- Gizzi, Michael. **Continental Harmonies**. 92p. $8.95.
- Goldman, Judith. **Vocoder**. 96p. $11.95.
- Gottlieb, Michael. **Ninety-Six Tears**. 88p. $5.
- Gottlieb, Michael. **Gorgeous Plunge**. 96p. $11.95.
- Greenwald, Ted. **Jumping the Line**. 120p. $12.95.
- Grenier, Robert. **A Day at the Beach**. 80p. $6.
- Grosman, Ernesto. **The XUL Reader: An Anthology of Argentine Poetry (1981–1996)**. 167p. $14.95.
- Hills, Henry. **Making Money**. 72p. $7.50. VHS videotape $24.95. Book & tape $29.95.
- Huang Yunte. **SHI: A Radical Reading of Chinese Poetry**. 76p. $9.95
- Hunt, Erica. **Local History**. 80 p. $9.95.
- Kuszai, Joel (editor) **poetics@**, 192 p. $13.95.
- Inman, P. **Criss Cross**. 64 p. $7.95.
- Inman, P. **Red Shift**. 64p. $6.
- Lazer, Hank. **Doublespace**. 192 p. $12.
- Levy, Andrew. **Paper Head Last Lyrics**. 112 p. $11.95.
- Mac Low, Jackson. **Representative Works: 1938–1985**. 360p. $12.95, $18.95 (cloth).
- Mac Low, Jackson. **Twenties**. 112p. $8.95.
- Moriarty, Laura. **Rondeaux**. 107p. $8.
- Neilson, Melanie. **Civil Noir**. 96p. $8.95.
- Pearson, Ted. **Planetary Gear**. 72p. $8.95.
- Perelman, Bob. **Virtual Reality**. 80p. $9.95.

- ❏ Perelman, Bob. **The Future of Memory.** 120p. $14.95.
- ❏ Piombino, Nick, **The Boundary of Blur**. 128p. $13.95.
- ❏ Raworth, Tom. **Clean & Will-Lit**. 106p. $10.95.
- ❏ Robinson, Kit. **Balance Sheet.** 112p. $11.95.
- ❏ Robinson, Kit. **Democracy Boulevard.** 104p. $9.95.
- ❏ Robinson, Kit. **Ice Cubes.** 96p. $6.
- ❏ Scalapino, Leslie. **Objects in the Terrifying Tense Longing from Taking Place.** 88p. $9.95.
- ❏ Seaton, Peter. **The Son Master**. 64p. $5.
- ❏ Sherry, James. **Popular Fiction**. 84p. $6.
- ❏ Silliman, Ron. **The New Sentence**. 200p. $10.
- ❏ Silliman, Ron. **N/O**. 112p. $10.95.
- ❏ Smith, Rod. **Protective Immediacy**. 96p. $9.95
- ❏ Stefans, Brian Kim. **Free Space Comix.**
- ❏ Tarkos, Christophe. **Ma Langue est Poétique—Selected Works**. 96p. $12.95.
- ❏ Templeton, Fiona. **Cells of Release**. 128p. with photographs. $13.95.
- ❏ Templeton, Fiona. **YOU—The City**. 150p. $11.95.
- ❏ Ward, Diane. **Human Ceiling**. 80p. $8.95.
- ❏ Ward, Diane. **Relation**. 64p. $7.50.
- ❏ Watson, Craig. **Free Will**. 80p. $9.95.
- ❏ Watten, Barrett. **Progress**. 122p. $7.50.
- ❏ Weiner, Hannah. **We Speak Silent**. 76 p. $9.95
- ❏ Wolsak, Lissa. **Pen Chants**. 80p. $9.95.
- ❏ Yasusada, Araki. **Doubled Flowering: From the Notebooks of Araki Yasusada.** 272p. $14.95.

ROOF BOOKS
are published by
**Segue Foundation, 303 East 8th Street, New York, NY 10009**
Visit our website at **segue.org**

Roof Books are distributed by
SMALL PRESS DISTRIBUTION
1341 Seventh Avenue, Berkeley, CA. 94710-1403.
Phone orders: 800-869-7553
**spdbooks.org**